Confessions

OF SCARRED

SOULS

Confessions of Scarred Souls
ISBN: 978-976-96117-0-2
Copyright ©2017 by Shaniqua L. Howell

Unless otherwise noted, all scripture quotations are from the New King James Version of the Bible. Copyright © 1982 by Thomas Nelson, Inc. Used by permission. All rights reserved.

Editor: Paula Richards - Eagle's Eye Editing Services
Email: eagleseyeservices@gmail.com

Cover Photo: @ Bess-Hamiti / www.Pixabay .com

SHELEV PUBLISHING
Email: Shelevpublishing@outlook.com
Telephone: 1 (246) 257-9611
Instagram: Shelevpublishing

Dedication

This book is dedicated to every person having a hard time trusting in the present because of the pain of the past. We have all been hurt and broken before, but never let it steal the flicker of hope in your heart. Keep the fire burning.

Declaration of a Scarred Soul

"I will be fine, and that's a given. Why? Because I know in whom I place my hope. I am positive that everything will work out according to His plan and purpose. Believing that God will come through for me is really not a problem, I know within my heart that He will not fail me, and for that I am very sure. But that doesn't mean the pain isn't fierce. To be honest, sometimes the pain is heavy, and I need a minute or maybe two, to catch my breath. I feel as if my heart is about to explode through my chest. BOOOMMM! What was a once calm heart is now rapidly beating.

I know what it feels like to look whole on the outside and be so crushed on the inside, but these problems of mine won't last forever; so despite I'm hurting so deeply, I am confident that God built me to withstand this storm. I am full of wounds, but I am still standing on my feet. I will ALWAYS hold on to the hand of God, trusting Him to bring me through this valley, and place me gracefully on the mountain top. I will not allow my worship to be circumstantial; so I will praise Him even when the walls are still standing. *"Abraham did not waver at the promise of God through unbelief but was strengthened in faith, giving glory to God."* (Romans 4:20) I too will strengthen myself in the Lord, giving all glory and honor to Him; I am confident that one day He will heal my scarred soul."

Contents

Introduction

Has your soul been scarred so deeply that you have sworn off love, and have now clung to bitterness? Don't die while you're still alive; you can overcome that which was sent to take you out; however, it's time to stop being a prisoner to your past. It's imperative that you don't allow the troubles of the past to color your present.

Life has a way of suffocating us at times; making us believe that the very air we are gasping for is unattainable. The death certificate has been written and the cause of death is 'trials and despair'. If this is you right now, then I need you to take a moment and rip up the report of the enemy.

Come with me and take a look into the true stories of men and women who came out on top despite the balls of discouragement life bowled at them. Pain is real and this cannot be negated, but God's power and healing are even more real than any hurt. I know it's heartbreaking right now and you feel like giving up and letting go. In your darkness you are unable to see a peep of light, but I encourage you to look again and see the light of God's SON shining down on your life. God healed these once scarred souls, and He can do the same for you. Put the spirit of determination into your stride. It was a lesson and not a death sentence. Your soul doesn't have to stay scarred; let God to do the mending and birth something breathtaking and purposeful out of the chaos you have experience.

Confession #1

Demon in Disguise

My story is the typical boy meets girl, boy tricks girl, and girl ends up with heartbreak, a tub of ice cream and a box of donuts. Women, be cautious; heartache can leave you with thunder thighs if you're not careful. I also allowed that junk food demon to trick me many times while dealing with the loss of "love". Why did I put love in quotation marks? Because I've come to realize that what I thought was love from past relationships, was just 'lust' subtly disguised as a form of love.

I've had some bad relationships, some weird ones at that, but I want to fast forward and get right to the crux of the matter. Let me introduce you to Devon, the one who caused me to be broken to the point where I thought I would never trust again. The one who made me seriously think about becoming a nun of the sorts. Well, maybe not. He was the one who I believed at the time, could very well have gone and sealed the deal with a 666 tattoo to confirm his status as a demon spawn, because surely he couldn't have been a Christian!

I met Devon at my church's youth rally and we instantly hit it off. His bubbly personality quickly caught my attention and it didn't hurt that he was tall, dark and handsome, and the brother really knew how to dress to impress. He seemed to love God, attended church every Sunday; he knew the Word, paid his tithes, was the head worship leader, Sunday school superintendent and he was always ready to help whenever he was needed. Everyone loved and believed in him, especially me. But who would have thought that it would all change with one text message? Certainly not me.

Our relationship was not perfect, but we were happy, I was very secure in what we had built for the past year, hoping he would soon ask for my hand in marriage. I even practiced my response many times in the mirror for the day when he would finally pop the question. Getting married and having kids had always been my dream and this was definitely it for me. I had found one of the good guys, and I was not letting him go.

I remember being in the kitchen washing dishes that fateful afternoon and hearing my phone alert me to the sound of an incoming message. I immediately washed my hands and ran to see who it was, as I was awaiting an email regarding a job I had applied for. I wasn't greeted with the good news I was eagerly seeking, instead, I was given information that stunned me in totality.

'Devon is gay. Come to Larry's restaurant at 1:00 pm and see for yourself.'

I stared at the phone for about ten minutes in utter shock and dismay. After pulling myself together upon hearing such disturbing information, I frantically dialed Devon's number but I got the voicemail. I glanced at my watch and saw that it was 12:30. If I wanted to get to Larry's for the time specified in the message, I needed to get moving and swiftly. With fear and confusion welling up on the inside of me, I grabbed my keys and headed out the door.

Up to this day, I'm not sure how I drove to the restaurant safely, because my mind was blank and I felt completely numb. The ride from the apartment to my destination was all a blur. I reluctantly dragged myself through the door when I arrived. Having visited the restaurant before, I asked the hostess for one of the seats in the back behind the aquarium. As I scanned the room, I saw no sign of Devon. "Good," I said to myself out loud. It meant that whoever was on the other side of that text message was a big fat liar, and I was not about playing games.

As I was getting up to leave the restaurant, I saw Devon walking behind the hostess who then directed him to a seat. My heart started to race sporadically. "Nooo…." I moaned softly, as I buried my face in my palms. This could not be true, I was not having it one bit. I needed answers and I needed them now! As soon as I found the strength to go over and confront him, I was taken back by what I saw. While trying to bring my anxiety under control, I did not notice that a man had joined Devon at his table.

I sat and watched my supposed boyfriend, make intimate gestures with a man. It made me sick to my stomach. The Bible speaks about righteous indignation, but that's not what I was feeling that day. I felt as if fire was blazing from my ears and nostrils. Tears refused to surface, but rage happily made its guest appearance. That same rage made me run across the other side of the restaurant toward Devon and his little friend, like a warrior on the battlefield charging at his opponent.

Luckily, two waiters were able to pull me off Devon and calm me before I made an even bigger spectacle of myself. By this time, his cheating accomplice had scampered off in fear. I later found out that Devon was living a double life and never had any plans on marrying me. He was simply using me as a cover in order to keep any suspicions of his homosexual behavior at bay. I had thought that he was a nice God-fearing man, only to find out that he was merely a demon in a very good disguise. A week had passed since the ordeal and I still had not yet shed one single tear. I was roused from my sleep one morning around 3:00 o'clock, and God spoke to me.

"I know you're not only angry at him but you're also angry with me. It's okay, just tell me how you feel and let it out."

I was mad at God and blamed Him for allowing me to incur such intense hurt. Of course, my finger was pointed in the wrong direction because it was not God's fault. But I desperately needed someone to blame other than myself. That night, I told God exactly how I felt and that's when the dam broke.

The journey to healing was not easy at all. There were times I wouldn't get out of bed and also times where I thought about seeking revenge, but I thank God for constantly saving and keeping me from myself. Psalm 147:3 states *"He heals the brokenhearted and binds up their wounds"* and that's exactly what the Lord did on my behalf. I was wounded, battered, bruised, hopeless and extremely brokenhearted. Then out of the blue, God spoke to me again.

"I have something in store for you, but you need to stop moaning and prepare yourself."

The Lord reminded me of the story of the potter's wheel in the book of Jeremiah chapter 18. His intent was never to punish me, but to create a masterpiece with my life. The transformation on the wheel was one of the most difficult times, but it had to be done. This was the place where God wanted to remove the impurities; the place where He needed to trim the old mindset and behaviors, so that I could walk in maturity and wisdom. It was necessary for my spiritual, emotional and mental growth.

About a year after my breakup with Devon, I met the current love of my life and fiancé. Up until that point, I had sworn off guys because of the disappointment I had endured. In my mind, I was not about to end up in the emergency room to be resuscitated again. NO WAY. I was focused on God and wasn't interested in going into a relationship, but God and Shane had other plans. He was not the type I preferred and he knew that from the start, but that never stopped him from pursuing me.

We were friends, and that's all I ever wanted it to be, until one day my true feelings started to tug at my heart. I got scared of going through another set of pain and betrayal, but God said *"It's okay, go ahead."* There I was, looking at the very thing I wanted for what seemed like an eternity, and yet I still refused to accept him, not only because of past hurt but also because he didn't look the way I had imagined.

How many times had I literally cried out to God like Jeremiah in the book of Lamentations for a true man of God? But when the time came and God answered my prayers, I wanted to run as far away as possible from the reality. It was too much to handle. Surely God was playing some kind of game with me, one I really wasn't interested in at that. Out of all the men on earth, he had to set me up with the shortest of them all.

After some long nights and days of debating and overthinking, I decided to trust God and give love another try. And it truly has been one of the best decisions I've ever made in my life. Yes, I was hurt and deceived, and spent many nights crying. Nevertheless, if I had not made the decision to forgive, heal and move on, I would not have my fiancé. I will forever thank him for never giving up on me even when I tried to push him away. His love is indeed unconditional and sacrificial, and I thank God every day for bringing him into my life.

Maybe you're at a place where you have been deceived and you feel as though your pain won't ever come to an end. Can I show you the way to your healing and restoration?

"Come to Me, all you who labor and are heavy laden, and I will give you rest. Take My yoke upon you and learn from Me, for I am gentle and lowly in heart, and you will find rest for your souls. For My yoke is easy and My burden is light." Matthew 11:28-30

Rest in God and place your burdened heart before Him. If I can make it through, then so can you. I know it hurts like hell, but I'm sure that if you decide to trust the Potter, He will turn your brokenness into a blessing. Maybe you've gone through the healing process but now you're at a place where you're afraid to let anyone back into your life. The only way to know if to trust again is by actually trusting again. It's okay to take risks, but use wisdom and always be guided by God. Don't allow your life to be one of stagnation. Someone may have scarred your soul, but it's either you stay wounded or change the route, heal and be made whole.

Confession #2

The Virtuous Woman

"Who can find a virtuous wife? For her worth is far above rubies."
Proverbs 31: 10

I have met many women who professed godliness, who professed to be Proverbs 31 women of virtue, yet their actions, speech, and character told a different story. The biblical standard of a virtuous woman is nothing like what we see in the world today; it's a rarity.

My very first relationship was at age 16; you may say that I was too young, but for me at that time, I had my life figured out, or so I believed. My grandmother was a woman of strong faith and she instilled in me Christian morals and principles, which made me the man I am today. While my peers were finding their joy in gangs, sex, violence or alcohol, I was finding my joy in God and doing His work. I was a peer counselor, part of the youth leaders group and president for the Inter-school Christian Fellowship.

Tammy was very supportive, and I believed within my heart that one day she would become my wife. Like I said before, I thought I had everything figured out; my plans just needed to go the way I wanted. We would graduate high school together, move on to college together and I would pop the question and ask her to marry me at graduation. Eventually we would marry and have a couple kids and live happily ever after. I really lived in a fantasy back then, because there was no happily ever after, but just an after without her in this story.

From the beginning of our relationship, I made it very clear that I was saving myself for marriage. She admired my position and agreed that we would not be sexually involved. There were times she would subtly say things that suggested she wanted to have sex, but I ignored them because she said purity was her goal. We spent most of our time together, but that all changed one day when she informed me that the printer at our school wasn't working so we decided to print our assignments in town the next day. When we were leaving the store, she proposed that we stop by her home as no one was there.

I was a 16-year-old male with desires; there was no way I was going to her house alone. Yes, I loved God and strived to live a life of purity, but wisdom should always prevail. The Bible speaks about fleeing temptation, and that's exactly what I did. I reminded her about our decision to save ourselves for marriage and tried my best to show her that it wasn't a good idea. I guess OUR decision was only my decision after all, because she walked away from me that day without saying a word. I knew she was upset, but surely she would see why we couldn't be alone.

Well, that day never came because she started to ignore me. After some time had passed, she was skipping school regularly and I felt as if I was to blame. But little did I know that it was because she was pregnant! I know, right? How could she possibly be pregnant when we never had sex? Her friends were the ones to tell me about her condition and even blamed me.

"How could you be a Christian and knock her up?"

Obviously, they were unaware of the situation because there was no way I could have been the father of her child. When I finally got a chance to confront her, she told me had I been handling my business, she would not have gotten pregnant. Was she serious? How could she say such a thing? Was she cheating all along? Did she even love me? Didn't we decide to wait?

My head was spinning with many questions and I wanted answers. I felt nauseous; I couldn't eat, I couldn't sleep and I felt like taking my life. Trusting another woman was going to be difficult, but for some reason I knew that I could trust God. When He said He loved me, it was a love without conditions. Despite my long days and sleepless nights, I turned to God and eventually chose to forgive her.

About a year after, I met Laura and we eventually got into a relationship. After the previous break up, I asked the Lord to help me to love without reservations. At the beginning, I exposed my heart and told her about my past hurt. I also informed her that I was still a virgin and had no plans on having sex before marriage and she happily obliged.

Nearly every day we studied and discussed the Word of God, and I was impressed with her knowledge and interpretation of scripture. I had a bit of hope; maybe this was finally it; someone who wanted to honor God. However, I was wrong yet again. One night while we were out on a date, we stopped by the park to relax, but things started to go south. The kissing, the touching, the groping; I was way in over my head.

"Stopppppp! I can't do this!" I yelled.

She was upset and said that nothing was wrong with what we were doing, but in my mind I knew it wasn't right. I was about to not only defile my temple, but hers as well. Kissing is not a sin, but it arouses the body and stirs up desires that kissing cannot satisfy. I've always believed in not compromising any part of my body or mind. Purity is a lifestyle; it is a direct instruction from God and what we were doing did not glorify God in anyway. I decided to call it a night and I headed home. I messaged her, but there was no response. The next morning I woke up to a text that sent me back to the place I never wanted to revisit – 'The Desert of Pain'.

Laura told me that she wouldn't be able to continue our relationship because her sexual needs were being deprived. I literally fell on my knees and started to cry out. Surely something was wrong with me. This was the second person who broke up with me because I refused to have sex. I recall my friends telling me that better would come. Better? There was no better; it seemed that they were all the same. Most women claimed they wanted a godly man, but did they? I was defeated, stressed and depressed yet again. This was now more painful than the first time. I had exposed my heart and soul to her and she basically did the same thing as Tammy.

Once again, I turned to Christ. It's encouraging to know that the God who made me can be trusted with the affairs of my life. We can expose our hearts to Him and He will never turn His back on us. Because of the pain, I built a wall around my heart and rejected anyone who tried their best to come in. Even though I had forgiven these people, I found myself trusting less and I was afraid of putting my heart out there to be trampled again.

At age 20, I met Amanda and decided that it was worth a try. She was deeply involved in church and also professed to be a virgin. This was really it then; she was a virgin and loved God, so she would definitely be serious about her purity. "Please, let this be it, God, "I begged.

Everything was going good until one night I went to town and saw her hugging another guy. A rush of anger rose up on the inside of me as I saw her giggling as he placed his hands around her waist. I scurried across the street to find out what was going on. When I confronted her and asked what she was doing, she said that he was her boyfriend. BOYFRIEND? So what was I? As the rain fell, I walked away in tears. She messaged me after some time and told me I was too nice and that's not what she was looking for. Déjà vu once again. Now I definitely knew that something was wrong with me. Why did it seem as if I was incapable of being loved?

My last encounter with pain was an eye-opener. She was once again very biblically sound. "I've been praying for a husband and your desires, qualities, and mentality are identical to what I've prayed for," she said. Despite the comforting words, she started to change and I saw a different person.

"You're way too nice and nobody likes that. You should be like Paul and just remain single; women these days want hardcore men," she blurted out one day.

I was confused. Wasn't this what she said she had prayed for? It's amazing how I hear women constantly say men are dogs, and that we are no good, but still on the other hand say that a person is too nice. I walked away from her and decided to put my all in God.

I never thought I would meet someone who was serious about honoring God wholeheartedly and who wouldn't want me to compromise my standards, but rather challenge me each day to walk in purity. In February 2017, I met such a woman in Miracle and I've grown to adore and appreciate her. She has inspired me to be a better man, and a better Christian. At this point, my desire is to one day make her my wife. What is so amazing to me is that even if we do not end up together, I am extremely grateful for the hope she has given me that godly women still do exist. To you woman of God, woman of virtue; I've met many women, but you surpass them all.

Looking back at the past, I am proud of myself for not compromising my beliefs. I am 23, still a virgin and have no intention of lowering my standards to please or satisfy anyone. My goal is to always please God. I have forgiven all of my exes and I can say today that I love them with God's love and even pray for the ones who have backslidden to return back to the faith.

If we want to heal, then we cannot hold onto the hurt of the past. Healing is a process and I am daily getting rid of anything that can affect my present or future. Instead of being bitter to those who hurt me, I looked at what I had instead of focusing on what I lost and it couldn't be compared. A blessing was concealed behind the sorrow. There is a simple but yet beautiful verse in a song that goes 'What can make me whole again, nothing but the blood of Jesus'. Jesus' blood has made me whole. It's His blood that heals, restores and delivers; give it all over to Him and watch what He can do for you.

Confession #3

Broken Doll

My soul wasn't scarred by a past lover like most stories in this book, but it was surely shattered by someone who made me question my very existence. I was a normal happy-go-lucky little girl who played with her Barbie dolls and enjoyed life without a care in the world. But that quickly changed and I was weighed down with a burden I was never meant to carry at such a tender age. I was clueless as to what was lurking in the shadows; Satan was hatching a plan for my life and the report read, 'Mental Annihilation', but I thank God continually for keeping me in my right frame of mind.

When it first started, I tried for a long time to put it at the back of my mind; I refused to believe I could be violated in such a manner. I figured that if I could make the thoughts go away, then it meant that it never happened. But it was impossible to forget —the smell, the touch, the whispers and breath of someone who completely invaded my privacy. To make it worse, it was someone I trusted.

When my mother took me to Aunty Dottie's house and the goodbyes were said, my torture commenced. Just like a predator ready to pounce on its prey in a National Geographic clip, my rapist, 'her son', awaited the opportunity to attack me as soon as his mother had disappeared from our sight.

Aunty Dottie had no idea that her son was a predator, and thus she would always ask him to help take care of me as he was older. There was a musty, broken down tool shed in their backyard, and that's where he took me in order to have his way with my body. That rust-filled, rat-infested garbage of a tool shed was the place where my virginity was taken away from me. The place where I completely felt as if I had died on the inside; where I screamed for help in my mind, but no one could hear me.

Where were my protectors, especially when I didn't even know I needed protecting? I prayer you understand how important it is to educate your children about their 'don't-touch' areas, and what they need to do if anyone ever touches them in the wrong manner. I do this with my children regularly; I will try my best to make sure they are never subjected to the misery that I experienced. No one, not even my parents spoke to me about molestation and because of that, I was easy prey.

Brandon repeatedly told me not to let anyone in on our little secret, and I never did. I grew up in a Christian home; Dottie and Brandon were also Christians, so why should I not trust what was going on? If I had known that what he was doing was wrong, I would have sung like a canary from the first time. The abuse would have never continued had I been educated, but it did. I was destroyed because of my lack of knowledge.

I, however, got older and came to the understanding that the abuse was not normal and that it was definitely not right, but at that point, I was too ashamed to tell. I remember one day watching a Lifetime movie with my mum and seeing her reaction to a child being sexually abused. I felt horrible, wondering how she would have reacted If I told her what was going on in my life. I sat next to her that night and bawled on the inside. If at any point she had said the slightest thing about it while watching the movie, I would have broken down and poured out my heart to her. But abuse never happened in Christian homes and to Christian people, right? So why would she have any reason to suspect anything of this nature was happening to her baby girl?

As the years rolled by, I tried my best to distance myself from him, but as 'fate' would have it, I was faced with another tormentor. As the older Bajan people would say, 'I ran from the frying pan straight into the fire'. My new tormentor was another person close to home; he was my aunt's friend's son. I want you to also understand that most of the time a child is being molested, it is usually from someone they know. Exercise discernment when it comes to having anyone around your children.

My cousins and I spent some time at my aunt's home and this is where he got the opportunity to hurt me. We always played hide and seek. Take a guess on who my hiding buddy was. Ding, ding, dinnngggg!! You are correct. NOT AGAIN! This could not be happening. It was as if I was a magnet for abuse. Why did this keep happening to me? How much more could a child possibly take? This was yet another person who took a piece of me and violated my trust. I was torn.

Because of the abuse I suffered at the hands of these boys, I was plagued with low self-esteem, rejection, and most of all, trust issues for a very long time. There was a tall brick wall of unforgiveness and I felt like it would never tumble down. They had violated me in every possible way and I believed with every fibre of my being that I had all rights not to forgive them. But God was not having that; forgiveness is hard, but it can be done. If a loving Father forgives me every single day, then why shouldn't I forgive when God said I ought to?

For if you forgive other people when they sin against you, your heavenly Father will also forgive you. But if you do not forgive others their sins, your Father will not forgive your sins. Matthew 6:14-15

When they say that God works in mysterious ways, my friend, you better believe it. I find it very ironic how I met Brandon's wife through work and now we are acquaintances. God loves to test us to see if we will not only talk the talk, but walk the walk. I honestly would not go out of my way to be friends with him, but I can say that I have no animosity or hatred towards him.

Today, I am married with three beautiful children and I am most grateful that I did not allow my broken heart to be a hindrance to me and my relationship with my husband. It could have gone down a different road and I could have allowed the bitterness to make me swear off men in general, but God is indeed a sustainer and a healer. He truly works out every sad and bad thing for those who love Him. They say that what God doesn't hinder, He allows. We may not always understand why bad things happen to good people, but know that God can bring you through any difficult situation and bring a blessing out of the betrayal.

I remember receiving a prophecy that I would help young women who have been through similar circumstances. How will I be able to help and nurture these women if I myself did not experience what they are going through? Just like Joseph, the enemy meant evil but God turned it around for my good and for the good of others who I will minister too.

My life is far from perfect; I have my personal struggles and moments, but I know that God will never leave me or forsake me even in my toughest, darkest, weakest and loneliest times. I turned my trauma into triumph; the dirt of my past will be used as manure to fertilize my future. Am I fully over the hurt? I believe so. Can I look into their faces and not remember what happened? Yes, I will remember; saying no would be a lie. Have I forgiven them? Yes, I have. Forgiveness is a choice and I will continue to choose to forgive. I refuse to give anyone the power to control me.

I know for a fact that the enemy sent out a hit against my life even at a young age because of the potential that lies on the inside of me. I should have lost my mind a long time ago, and probably ended up in the psychiatric hospital, but God's assignment was more powerful than the enemy's plot. I am not just a conqueror, but I'm more than a conqueror. The broken pieces of my once shattered soul and life have been glued back together again and made even better than before. I am not a victim; I am a victor.

Confession #4

A Husband Scorned

Charles Spurgeon said: *"Whenever God means to make man great, he always breaks him into pieces"*. Boy, was I broken into a million pieces. I grew up in church all my life and my mother made sure that my sister and I were there every Sunday, even if there was a thunderstorm. And I'm not kidding. In my teenage years I grew tired of the restraints in our household, and at this point the worldly things started to look exciting to me. My interest was piqued, and there was no stopping me. Yes, I loved God, but I wanted to explore a world that was forbidden, just as Eve did in the garden. Curiosity got the best of me; one foot was in the church and the other in the world, not knowing that I was making myself an enemy of God.

> *Adulterers and adulteresses! Do you not know that friendship with the world is enmity with God? Whoever therefore wants to be a friend of the world makes himself an enemy of God.* James 4:4

At the age of 19, my girlfriend told me she was pregnant; we were both ecstatic but on the other hand I was terrified. I wasn't sure how my parents would feel about Amy being pregnant. I thought that maybe I would be a disgrace to them. Their good, young intelligent Christian son, as they called me many times, had made a mistake and gotten his girlfriend pregnant; what would their friends think? Amidst the shock of it all, to my surprise, they were very supportive of my girlfriend and our baby. We welcomed a beautiful baby girl into our family the next year and we pretty much continued with our lives.

When my daughter was about three years old, I felt a sense of unease and became restless in my spirit. God was calling me back to Him and I could not shake the feeling. Where fornication was easy and fun before, it now became a thorn in my flesh and I always felt the conviction of the Holy Spirit. I recommitted my life to the Lord and told Amy that I could no longer live in sin and that we needed to get married. I wanted to do right by God and so I thought at the time that it was the right decision. She was not on the same path to Christ as I was, but I believed that one day she would accept Jesus as her Savior.

After we got married, my son then came and I was happy. After a couple years into the marriage, things started to take a turn for the worse. I saw the changes in my wife for a long time, but I swept many things under the carpet continuously without addressing them, until it was too much to handle.

We would have disagreements about her not wanting to go to church and the fact that she was a bit too flirty with the opposite sex, but I loved her and I wanted to make my marriage work at all costs. Breaking up my family was never an option. I suspected, however, that Amy was up to no good, but I never had the evidence to prove that anything was going on. She always made excuses for the lies I would catch her in. Maybe I was just being paranoid, I tried to tell myself.

Suspecting something leaves you with a feeling of anxiousness, but actually finding out your suspicions are true is horrifying. I found text messages that proved Amy was cheating and it split my heart in two. I confronted her about what I saw, but yet again, she made excuses and denied she was having an extramarital affair. The little attention that she was giving me had gone to zero and it cut deep.

I was neglected and alone, the rejection was strong and it opened another door for the enemy to reap havoc in my marriage. There was a young woman named Linda who I saw on occasions when I delivered items to her workplace. She would always flirt with me, but I never give her the time of day. But things took a different turn. She gave me the attention that I craved from my wife and I was a goner.

I started having an affair just like my wife. I acted out of the pain and it led to a behavior that was out of character. I had been faithful to her even before we were married and I was devastated that she could hurt me that way. I wanted her to experience the pain I was feeling, to hurt the way I was hurting and so I found comfort in the arms of another woman. I pleaded with her many times for us to work on our marriage, but it was to no avail. She continued denying her affair even though I had all the evidence. I wasn't getting the satisfaction I wanted and so I continued in my sin as she continued to ignore and reject me. I became promiscuous, and even started partying, but never once did I stop going to church.

Out of the blue, Amy informed me that she was going abroad to work for a while and she was leaving the kids with me. My shouts and tantrums did not make a difference because within two weeks she was gone. She hadn't only left me alone, but she left our children as well. What mother does that? I was devastated. Hearing the cries of my children every day for their mother, made me all the more mad at her.

Rumors were circulating that she was pregnant, but I refused to believe it. When she would call to speak to the kids I would ask about it, but she would always deny the accusations. I was facing another set of rejection. How could someone pack their bags and leave their family without a care in the world? Despite her saying she was going abroad to work, I never received a penny for the children. I begged her many times to come back home. Even telling her that if she was pregnant, I wouldn't mind, I just wanted her back. I was willing to do anything to keep my family together, but she said she wasn't ready to return. I continued to have a sexual relationship with Linda. I knew it was wrong on so many levels, but I felt hopeless and I wanted someone to want me. We were both having an extramarital affair; there was no way God was happy about what either of us was doing.

People were asking questions, snickering and making comments about my wife. At this point, she was gone for about a year. She then returned home, but she wasn't alone, she did have a baby and it wasn't mine. I thought that I couldn't possibly hurt any worse but I was wrong. Amy told me she didn't want to be with me and she then moved in with the father of her baby. I read a quote somewhere on the internet that said "If someone doesn't want you it's not the end of the world, but if you do not want yourself, that's the end of your world and the beginning of self-destruction – emotionally and mentally."

By this time, I was sinking deeper into depression; if it had not been for God and my beautiful children to give me just that smile each day, I don't know what I would have done. Those were the roughest days I've ever experienced in my life, but somehow God kept me through it all. I almost lost my mind, I almost had a nervous breakdown, but God didn't allow it.

I got so tired of living the life I was living; a life full of hurt, disappointment, bitterness and anger. I met back up with Karen who I knew from my teenage church days. I believe people come into our lives for a reason and according to the seasons that we're going through. She came into my life and helped me on the path back to Jesus. I cut off the relationship with Linda and I stopped partying and partaking in ungodly behavior. She was an encourager and someone I could open up to about what I was going through. I believe God placed her in my life at that time to help me get my act together. I was back in the arms of my Creator and it felt so good; just like the prodigal son, I had returned home and recommitted my life once again, but this time it was for good.

When I eventually saw Amy and her new baby, I felt such peace compared to the rage I felt for her before. I was now able to communicate without cussing her out or becoming flustered. I guess Jesus knew what could have possibly gone wrong, so He came to my rescue before I ended up writing this behind bars when I saw the guy she cheated on me with (Lol).

One of my friends connected me with his friend who was a lawyer. What could have taken months and then years to process with the numerous court days and hearings, only took a couple of weeks. Many marriages have been restored after the betrayal of adultery, but in my situation that wasn't the outcome. I was always willing to put in the work, but it was not the case on both sides. I had no choice but to let go and walk away.

Today, I can boldly say that God has kept me even in my disobedience; there isn't any sin too big for Him to forgive. I was made whole again; God showed up in the mess and I'm forever grateful. When I forgave Amy, I began to see things change in my life. We are amicable in dealing with our children and her son even calls me uncle and my children love their brother. The Bible speaks about a peace that surpasses all understanding and that is what I've experienced.

I am a different person today; I am stronger, wiser and my faith in God is way bigger. My heart is now free for the love I know God will one day bless me with. God has brought me from some horrible places, but I know the ugly parts of my story will be used for someone's breakthrough. I emptied my hold on unforgiveness and bitterness so that I can catch everything God has in store for me. My story has just begun.

Confession #5

With This Ring!

"I, David, take you Alicia, to be my lawfully wedded wife, to have and to hold, from this day forward, for better, for worse, for richer, for poorer, in sickness and in health. I promise to love, honor and cherish you until death do us part."

As much as those vows meant the world to me, they never meant anything to the man who promised on our wedding day to cherish me for the rest of our lives. David was wanted by nearly every woman who laid eyes on him. Six feet, five inches tall, chiseled frame, smooth vanilla complexion and a smile that showed his dimples and white teeth. He was a successful businessman who knew how to seal a deal with anyone in three minutes tops. Whenever he spoke, his words were always sweeter than honey, and that's how he was able to talk me straight to the altar even though he was unsaved. Proverbs 5:3-4 speaks about the immoral woman;

well, he was my immoral man. "For the lips of an immoral woman drip honey and her mouth is smoother than oil." I fell in love with his words, but unfortunately, he was a good liar. I was distracted by the way he was formed and missed what he was filled with, and it wasn't God he was full of.

I had encountered some horrible relationships with some "so-called Christian men", so by the time I met David, I was grieved by the men in church who couldn't seem to get their act together. Why not give David a chance? He was sweet, kind, loving and he was interested in me. What could possibly go wrong? Why should I shoo him away just because he did not attend church every Sunday?

My thinking was completely messed up at the time. I could not see, or should I say, I refused to see because I was tired of being the only single person among my friends. I was fed up with the process of the wait and allowed Satan to distract me with his counterfeit ideal man. How can two walk together unless they agree? The Bible is crystal clear about being unequally yoked, and no human excuse can be used to stamp out the Word of God. If you're currently dating, courting or engaged to someone who is unsaved, I urge you to not commit yourself to a marriage covenant; you are knowingly being rebellious to God. Do not yoke yourself together with darkness.

David hardly ever came to church and that was fine with me; he understood that I wanted to wait until marriage to have sex, and that made me believe he was honorable. "Ohhhhhh Pleaseeeee." Men like my ex-husband are very strong-willed when it comes to getting what they want. They will exercise patience on many levels in order to receive their prize.

My mentor pleaded with me many times not to marry, but I was having none of it. When we search through scriptures, there are many accounts of people receiving wisdom from godly counsel. Yes, there are times, when we have to do like Jesus and say "get thee behind me Satan" as He did with Peter. A person may be saying the right thing but it may not be the thing God wants for us. However, we ought to listen when we are given advice from people who may see what we cannot. Sometimes we are blinded by lust and this is where our friends, family members, and spiritual leaders can help us make good decisions (Proverbs 15:22).

I ignored the concerns of the people around me and went ahead and tied myself to Satan's son. I should have said, "If you don't want anything to do with the God I serve then you don't want anything to do with me." But I didn't. Within a year and a half of us being together, we got married and that was the day my life as I knew it, ended.

The loving, caring and gentle man, turned into a beast who had been unleashed from his chains seeking blood. Two weeks into marriage I started to see the other side of my husband. One day we were arguing about him working regularly and he lashed out at me. I was slapped repeatedly across the face and told that I needed to shut up. Shock was not the word to describe how I felt at the time. As I stood there holding my face crying, I saw the coldness in his eyes and knew I had made a mistake at the altar. However, it was too late.

Like any abuser, he apologized and said that it would never happen again. But it did, it always did. For years I suffered, physical, verbal and emotional abuse at the hands of the man who said he loved me. I did not know where to turn or what to do; I wasn't comfortable enough to confide in anyone because I was always afraid of my husband finding out and me having to pay the price. I was also ashamed to go to the very people tried to warn me.

My relationship with God was stifled and I stopped going to church all together. I went outside the will of God because I was tired waiting on a husband, so I had to stay outside His will to keep it. When we were out in public we were the perfect couple, but behind those lovely, big, expensive doors, I was living hell on earth.

David wanted a child, but as much as we tried I never got pregnant. We went to every doctor we could find, and they all said the same thing. I was fine, but still we never conceived. Looking back, I knew it was God. I only wanted a child in order to please him, thinking that it would somehow lessen the beatings and the verbal abuse. But every time I thought about bearing a baby for him, I would cringe. Every chance he got he made me feel like less of a woman because I could never get pregnant. He wanted something and I wasn't able to give him, and he made sure I knew how disgusted he felt.

A little bit of heaven touched down on my house when David's niece and her six-year-old daughter came to stay with us. She was going through a rough time and needed a place to rest her head until she was able to get back on her feet. Nicole was a little distant and antisocial, but she never gave me any reason to be suspicious of her in anyway. Her daughter Ariel brought a warmness to our home, and me and my husband doted on her. Having them there with us did wonders on his attitude; the abuse wasn't over, but it had lessened.

Many times I swore I saw Nicole scoff when David and I were together, but I always shoved it at the back of my mind. Maybe she felt alone after having found out she was pregnant and would be a single parent of two. I prayed countless nights that Nicole wouldn't leave; my husband and I were financially able and our house was big enough for all of us. Once she pulled her weight around our home, I would be grateful. David was happier than usual and that meant life was better for me.

About six months after Nicole moved into our home, my friends were having a getaway weekend at The Marriott Hotel; with encouragement from David, I decided to go and have some down time. Fortunately for me on the first night, I caught a stomach bug from something I ate and decided to call it quits and go home earlier than scheduled. The girls had planned this weekend for a long time and I didn't want to be the one to ruin it with my sickness. You're probably wondering how sickness could be fortunate, but you will soon find out why; just hang tight.

Upon reaching home that night, I had the weirdest feeling that my life was about to change. I opened the door, dropped my bags in the hallway and hurried to our master bathroom to empty my stomach once again. I didn't want to bother David by turning on the lights, so I fumbled around in the darkness.

When I opened our bedroom door, the scrambling alerted me to the fact that something was up. I quickly flicked on the lights and tried to make sense of what was going on.

Beads of sweat immediately started to form over my nose and eyes. My saliva had formed so thick in my mouth that I felt as if I was choking and I was lost for words. I was standing there, but I felt like I was on another planet. It was as if I had been thrown overboard a moving boat. I was drowning, the water was overtaking me, oxygen levels were starting to decrease, and the more I struggled, the more difficult it was to breathe. I was going under.

"Breathe, Alicia, breathe." I was now coaching myself back to reality.

It was difficult for me to believe the picture before my eyes. My husband was in our bed having sex with Nicole. Words still failed to escape my mouth as I stood there in astonishment. They never heard me pull into the driveway because they were too busy getting it on. How could he disrespect me like that? In addition, why was he having sex with his own niece? I felt repulsed and despondent.

"Are you guys crazy?"

I found my voice, but to my amazement they both acted nonchalant. Nicole had the widest smirk on her face as if she was enjoying every bit of the production. I truly felt like slapping her into the next week, but I quickly remembered that she was pregnant. David snarled at me and asked that I leave the room immediately. I was baffled. Leave the room? Was I hearing right? He was telling me to leave our room, for him to continue to have sex with his flesh and blood? I was fed up; I had had enough, I reached my breaking point and I snapped.

I calmly walked away from the bedroom door and headed to the kitchen where I saw an empty wine bottle, which more than likely they had been drinking earlier. Without thinking, I took up the bottle and charged back into the bedroom and hit David over the head until he collapsed on the bed. Nicole screamed and ran for dear life, but this wasn't about her; I didn't care that she got away. I was focused; I wanted to annihilate the man who I gave my life and my body to, but he still saw it fit to disrespect me in my home.

David laid motionless on the bed, as the blood ran down his head. The room looked like a scene from CSI Miami; the sheets were covered in blood and pieces of glass were everywhere. I finally snapped out of my anger and immediately went into panic mode. My heart was racing as I thought the worst. Was he dead? Was I going to jail?

"Ohhh Goddd! Help me!" I cried.

I ran over to David and shook him in order to wake him up; eventually he came out of his unconscious state and I let out a sigh of relief. As I sat there on the bedroom floor that night waiting for the ambulance to come, I opened up my mouth and did what I hadn't done in a very long time. I prayed; I asked God to save my husband as I didn't want him to die at my hands. I repented right there and asked for forgiveness. All the years of bottled hurt came out in rage, and caused me to bring harm to another individual. I cried like a baby not only for him to be alright, but for me to be alright as well.

My husband suffered a minor concussion and refused to press charges despite the promptings of the police. I filed for a divorce and he willingly let me go without a fight. It turned out that Nicole was not his niece and her two children were actually his. He had brought his mistress into our home and that hurt me to the very tip of my toes. I went through a process of counseling and deliverance in order to put the pieces of my life back together. I recommitted my life to God and allowed Him to mend my broken heart and heal my tainted soul.

My situation made me run into the arms of my Savior, the very place where I needed to be and should have never left. Countless times I woke up in the middle of the night screaming. There were times when I couldn't fall asleep on my own and needed to take prescription pills. There were also times that I wanted to kill myself so the suffering would stop. But I thank God every day for keeping me; I had left Him but He never left me. My healing did not come at an easy price, but it was worth it. This is one of the scriptures that helped me through it all.

I shall not die, but live, and declare the works of the Lord. Psalm 118:17

Yes, I have been wounded, but I'm still here and that's a living testimony of God's goodness. I shall surely live and not die to declare the works of the Lord. My prayer for you is to not fall into the same trap as I did. Don't say 'I do' to the person God said 'don't' to. For some of you, I feel in my spirit as if God wants you to take a step back from the relationship you're currently in so you can see the red flags. The truth may hurt now but it will save you later. Ask the Lord to keep you focused on what He sends your way and not what you think is sent from Him. Marriage is the next biggest decision you will ever make after salvation, so I implore you to be wise in your choosing.

I have forgiven David and Nicole, but I believe that God isn't finished with me yet. I've come a mighty long way from where I was, but I know that He wants to do some more pruning and refining in my life. I'm still young and strong, so I believe there is a love somewhere out there for me. In the meantime, I'm working on me. I thank the Lord today for the trials that nearly took me out. I wanted to throw in the towel many times, but God kept throwing it back at me. The process isn't always easy, but what it produces in the end is spectacular.

Confession #6

Love Triangle

I have kissed a few frogs in my lifetime, but none of them could have prepared me for kissing a goat. Maybe my words are a little harsh, but that's exactly how I felt. I thank God every day for placing His hand on my life, and dissolving my 'situationship' into nothing. Yes, I said it! 'SITUATIONSHIP!' Because that's exactly what it was. God uses trials to teach us to take our hands off the things that are not secure and to place them on the only thing that is — and that's Him.

I knew Zeke from my college days and we would always greet each when passing the halls. There was mischief behind his eyes, which led me to believe that he was a player. I had a sense that he wanted it to go further than our small conversations, but I wasn't fond of him at the time. After a couple years, we met up again and started chatting via Facebook. The more we talked, the more I was drawn to him, but despite those feelings, something didn't feel right in my spirit. Thinking I was just being paranoid, I mentioned it to one of my friends who said it was probably just all in my mind. But it wasn't. Putting what I summed up to be paranoia on the back burner so to speak, I continued to develop a friendship with Zeke.

God was chasing me down while waving those red flags trying to get my attention, but I did not take heed. My first visible red flag with Zeke happened on the night of a function he informed me he was attending. I asked if he was going alone and of course he said yes, but I didn't believe him. Just like Spider Man on the trail of a villain, my spidey senses were tingling. So what did I do, you ask? I quenched the thirst of my suspicion and I went to the function unknown to him.

I got there just in time to see him exiting the event with his ex-fiancé, looking rather cozy. As soon as he took her to her car, he called and asked what I was doing. Enraged, I called him a liar and a cheater based on what I had seen, but he denied they were together and said he was merely making sure she got to her car safely. Maybe I had misjudged the situation and was too quick to assess what was happening? I figured that was the case, so I convinced myself that everything wasn't what it appeared to be and I chose to forgive him, but I still couldn't bring myself to trust him completely.

About two months after the episode, I sensed that God wanted me to break it off with Zeke and so I did. He was hysterical and thought I was insane for ending our relationship as his intentions were to marry me. I continued with the plan of calling it quits, but that didn't last for too long, because after three weeks, he called and we decided to continue our relationship. It's so comforting to know that God cares so much about our well-being, that He takes the time to prompt us continually to save us even when we choose to ignore Him. And I was definitely ignoring Him.

I remember having a dream that we were on our way to the airport to travel, but as soon as we got on the plane, it crashed. I was unsure why I had the dream and what it meant at the time. God had been nudging me all along, but I kept thinking it was just me being paranoid. You're probably saying by now, "OMG, this girl is definitely dumb." Why did I continue to go back with this dude even though God was taking me left because he wasn't my 'Mr. Right? It's sad to say that in my confused state, I allowed my emotions to lead me instead of allowing God to guide me. It happens to the best of us.

My best friend told me he saw Zeke with another female, but once again he denied it, along with the fake tears. If he had ever auditioned for Broadway, I am convinced that he would have gotten the lead role; the dude was full blown dramatic. I kept telling myself that the good little Christian boy who led worship and talked about how much he loved God would never cheat on the woman he said he wanted to marry. This was the guy I loved, so I had to believe that he was incapable of cheating.

In the summer of 2016, I caught Zeke in a very disturbing situation and up to this day I cannot fathom what I actually saw. He said he was going to bed, but as usual he was acting a bit weird and so I decided to go to his house. YESSSS! Call me Sherlock Holmes because I was on the case immediately. I found myself skeptical of everything he said and did, and this time it wasn't any different.

When I got to his home, a sleeping Zeke was not what I found. As I peeped through the living room window, I saw what no woman should ever have to see in her life; her partner in a compromising situation with a bunch of his male friends. I scampered back to my car and drove back home that night bewildered. I was trying my best to remove the images of Zeke being intimate with his "friends" from my mind but it was impossible.

The weight of the hurt was heavy on my chest; I had questions and I wasn't sure if I wanted the answers. He had said he loved me, but his mouth was full of lies. I thought I had prepared myself for him cheating on me with another woman, but never did I imagine a man. I was rendered speechless. He was really Zeke the Freak. The next day I told him I no longer wanted to be in the relationship. I didn't see the need to invest my heart and time into someone who was clearly demented; He had problems being faithful and didn't have a clue what the word trustworthy meant.

I later found out from reading his emails that he was sleeping with other women, one of whom he married after we broke up. Knowing that I had access to his passwords, it was stupid of him to leave such evidence behind. On reading each conversation, the hatred increased, and I wondered on many occasions how I would make it to the other side of the pain. I even thought about confronting his soon-to-be wife and putting a stop to their wedding by telling her about his cheating ways and bisexual tendencies. But I didn't need to worry about him anymore; we were over. I needed to work on me.

Just like blind Bartimaeus in Mark chapter 10, I cried out for Jesus to heal me because I knew it was impossible for me to heal myself. Desperation is the key for our restoration and we need not be ashamed to cry earnestly before the Lord.

My flesh and my heart fail; but God is the strength of my heart and my portion forever. Psalm 73:26

My flesh and my heart failed me, but God kept reminding me that He is the strength of my heart and my portion forever. He never promised a life without heartache, but His Word promised me hope in the difficult times. I had to trade the hurt in order to get to my healing; it was a difficult swap but it was necessary. As I look around and see men continue to rip the hearts out of women, it upsets me. If only the church would prepare men to be husbands as much as they strive to prepare women to be wives. Zeke had compromised my perception of men, and for a while I didn't think it was possible for me to love again. I had to silence the whispers that said I wouldn't find true love.

Pain changes people in different ways; it can make you trust less and shut people out. It's okay to be cautious, but it's never okay to cut yourself off from love because some idiot did you dirty. Sometimes the hardest part about being a great catch is accepting that not everybody's hands are strong enough to hold you. Zeke made me realize that some men, depending on their level of maturity, are not ready for marriage.

I never thought I would be able to forgiven him, but I have. He didn't only break my heart he had broken my spirit as well; my heart had physically hurt for months, but I'm better now. Though I'm not ready for a relationship, I'm open to what God will do in my life someday. I strive towards complete healing and I can truly say I still believe in love and I await my Prince! I now ask God to show me who to meet and who to miss. We get to decide if our trials will define us or make us better versions of ourselves, and I wanted to learn from the lessons and not have them destroy me.

Whenever you think you're interested in someone, put their name in the place of 'love' in 2 Corinthians chapter 13. This is the kind of love God expects from us and Zeke possessed none of them.

Love suffers long and is kind; love does not envy; love does not parade itself, is not puffed up; does not behave rudely, does not seek its own, is not provoked, thinks no evil; does not rejoice in iniquity, but rejoices in the truth; bears all things, believes all things, hopes all things, endures all things. 1 Corinthians 13:4-7

I want to leave you with one of the deepest things you will ever hear in life: Never ignore the nudging of the Holy Spirit. If I had done this, it would have saved me from plenty heartache. The best mistakes you can learn from, is someone else's mistakes, so learn from mine.

Confession #7

He Kept Me

I felt as if someone had pulled the rug from under me, leaving me with bruises I thought would never heal. "What I am doing you do not understand now, but you will know after this" (John 13:7). This was what the Lord said to me when my world felt as if it had collapsed. He knew I would be frustrated and confused. He knew I wouldn't understand and that I would have doubts, but he was asking me to trust His plan because His plan was to prosper me spiritually, financially, emotionally and to fill my life with hope and an incredible future.

We were best friends before we became lovers; everything we did, we did together. After being thrown out of my mother's home, he and his family readily welcomed me in. He had a beautiful little girl that I saw as my own and we had a son together who we absolutely adored; it felt like we were a match made in heaven. Yes, we had our arguments, but within a few hours we would look to each other and ask, "What were we arguing about?" or by sunrise, we were cuddled up together. But while we, or should I say 'I thought we' were both brainstorming on our next move together as a family, those dreams and plans suddenly came crashing down.

It was after I started to attend church that our relationship got rocky. He made it clear that he wasn't about the "church life", so while I was at church, he found other things to occupy his time; and while he was pulling further away from me, I was getting closer to God. This was my best friend, the one who knew my darkest secrets, who knew my fears, who I had loved, but there was something about this God and I wanted to get to know Him. So despite his feelings towards the church, I continued to pursue a relationship with the Lord, even though it wasn't the best at the time.

During a conversation with a friend, she mentioned she had seen Dominic with a woman. The description of the person she saw at the time wasn't quite accurate, but though he denied and bitterly argued that the person needed to mind their business, something within me felt that there was some truth to the story. As time went by, things started to change for the worse. I would fall asleep at night waiting for him to come home, then I would wake up in the wee hours of the morning only to discover that he was not in bed. I would repeatedly call his cell, never getting an answer, only to be later told fibs such as "I forgot the phone in the car" or "the phone was on silent". Riiiiight!

You may be saying, if I felt or knew there was someone else why didn't I leave? But, I loved what I knew to be family; that was all I had. I feared not being able to make it on my own, or most of all having to return to my mom. That wasn't an option. So I tried. I tried to mend what I knew had been broken, but all my efforts were in vain.

It takes two willing people to make a relationship work. You see, it is quite easy for one to cling to something that's new and fresh. It's like being given a new car to drive, fully loaded, free insurance, free road tax, free gasoline for a year; I'm certain you may opt to park or sell your old vehicle for that smooth drive on the bumpy roads. Those nights of trying to talk things through just felt like every road I turned there were more potholes; argument after argument. After a while I dreaded going home because I knew I would be greeted with another argument once he was there. It was evident that he wanted to trade in the old car (me) for the new shiny sports car (his affair).

One night, I awoke to a voice. It was the voice of God. "Tori, Tori, get up and go home." I knew God meant back home with my mom. I was dumbfounded as to why I had to leave and the tears gushed from my eyes. I wasn't ready to give up and let it all go. I didn't obey the voice of God that night; instead I turned over to Dominic to question him. "What did I do? Is there someone else? Did you have sex with her?" I was willing to forgive him for whatever he had done to keep our family together. My emotions felt like a kite attempting to dance through a hurricane.

Emotional pain, if not treated, can be the root problem to a number of our physical ailments. Sharp and sudden pains were felt in my lower abdomen. I visited the family doctor, but there were no abnormalities found, so I tried having a blood analysis done, hoping they would be able to tell me what was going on with my body. Dr. Simmons recognized that there was some emotional pain, which I needed to deal with before recommending me to see the gynecologist.

While I was looking for a physical reason for the pain, he believed it ran much deeper than that. Eventually I saw the gynecologist and she thought it best to have a laparoscopy to ensure nothing was there. The physical examinations and further blood tests weren't picking up anything. My sickness wasn't as long as the woman with the issue of blood, but it left me drained mentally, physically, and financially.

Sharing the news with Dominic didn't matter, it was like talking to a brick wall, or maybe I would have had a better response from the wall than I was getting from him. It was that bad. We didn't fight with our hands, but the words were harsh, they cut to the bone. The saying "Sticks and stones will break my bones, but words will never harm me" is a lie; especially if those words are spoken by someone you love.

The fights were getting to the point where I started to think about going back with my mom, but I quietly dismissed the thought. However, after the words "I'm sick and tired of you" came one Saturday morning when I called him at work, I found the courage I didn't know I had to visit my mom and ask her if I could come home. Without hesitation she said yes. So I packed my things and prepared for my journey without the very person I ached for. I daydreamed about him rushing home from work and telling me not to leave, but that was just one of those dreams that would never come through. Instead of feeling regretful about me leaving, he went out with his friends as I packed the truck to leave.

I was broken, ashamed and embarrassed as persons informed me he was out with another woman immediately after I had moved out. I felt double-crossed. However, he continued with the lies; he denied everything, but I knew it was only a matter of time before the truth would show its face. Until then, I had to sit it out and wait. As my granny would always say, "You can hide and buy land, but you can't hide and work it."

My friends were cruel with their remarks as I was trying to hold myself together. "Get over it, why are you sulking behind a man? It isn't like you guys were married." I felt utterly helpless and alone. People fail to understand that a breakup can be very painful. After being with Dominic for almost half my life, I thought I deserved the right to grieve. We need to be careful with the way we speak to others when they are grieving because it can push them to the edge and maybe to the edge of a cliff, literally. Everyone mourns differently and we should be considerate about that, giving them the space and the right to grieve.

Many people not knowing what was going on would enquire about my weight loss program; I had gone from a size ten to a six within weeks. I wanted to will the pain away but it wasn't happening; if I could have just died I figured the pain would then go away. My eyes were puffy and red from ever-flowing tears day and night; I used alcohol and medication in hopes of getting rest. I actually started to believe that I was the reason for his disinterest.

Sunday after Sunday, I found myself at the altar bawling like a baby, just asking God to help me through it all. At times I became angry with Him because shortly after accepting Him as my Lord and Savior, everything in my life had fallen apart. Well, according to me it was, but I failed to understand at the time that it was all going according to His divine purpose. "Why God? Why? You said you wouldn't give me more than I could bear, but this is too much."

If I had thought that it was too much, there was about to be more; the woman he claimed he wasn't with, ended up pregnant. "Lord!" I cried, "You give the hardest battles to the strongest soldiers, and I'm not strong enough. This pain is too much. How am I supposed to handle this now on top of everything?" I never believed that a child or children should suffer if the relationship of the parents was broken, and I didn't want it for my own. I never spoke any bad or negative words about their father because I knew that one day they would be old enough to put the pieces together and understand.

As time went by, the dreams or should I say the nightmares started. I understood somewhat how irritated Hannah felt with Penninah parading with her bump she carried for Elkanah in the book of 1 Samuel. I said somewhat, because I didn't experience it in the natural, I never saw her while she was pregnant, but the dreams felt just as real. I thought her pregnancy was it, but Satan has a way of adding more fuel to the fire to set it ablaze. I tried to brace myself for the baby's arrival, but never did I think that it would be a pre-birthday "present". I could not even celebrate my birthday.

Stop whining you may say, or she's overly dramatic, but I won't expect you to understand unless you've walked the journey yourself. Maybe I needed to be dramatic first before I got over it. Those of you who have or are going through, I sympathize with you. God said in Isaiah 41:10, "Fear not, for I am with you; Be not dismayed, for I am your God. I will strengthen you, Yes, I will help you, I will uphold you with My righteous right hand." I'm not saying that it will be miraculously over by tomorrow but, "Being confident of this very thing, that He who has begun a good work in you will complete it until the day of Jesus Christ" (Phil 1:6). Through the tears I had to learn to trust God and He started a good work in me.

"Forgive him and pray for them," He said.

"Really God?" My heart instantly hardened.

"Yes!" He responded promptly.

"But I say to you, love your enemies, bless those who curse you, do good to those who hate you, and pray for those who spitefully use you and persecute you" (Matthew 5:44). It took me a while; yes, it was difficult, but eventually I did. When I made that choice to forgive, it became easier, even for baby Rory. If I believed that God knew me before I was formed in my mother's womb, sanctified me and ordained me a prophet to many nations, then the same applied to baby Rory. He too was chosen.

Forgiveness is the antidote for spiritual freedom. For if you forgive people their sin, their wrong doings, whatever they have done to cause you pain, then your heavenly Father will also forgive you. Refusing to forgive, leaves you destined to live a life filled with anger, bitterness, hurt, resentment; a life of misery and most importantly, in a state where your heavenly Father will not forgive you either.

Over time, God healed me completely. I have what I have and I'm happy; I lost what I lost and I am still happy. I have no regrets today about the years I spent with Dominic because I gained my children from our relationship. Neither do I regret our breakup because my relationship with God would not have grown into the beauty it is today. I can see now that God was bringing me to Himself because he wanted me for Himself, but my mind was on Dominic. I guess you can say he was an idol.

Steven Furtick said, *"God allows us to go through the exact experiences He wants us to have in order to shape the specific destiny He's designed for us."* The hurt wanted to make me give up on love; it stifled me for a time, but now my heart is open to a love that God will one day gift me. I faced the fiery trials with faith; I am not my scars.

Confession #8

Unchecked Emotions

Everyone experiences the hurt of a broken relationship at some point in their lives. I wouldn't say that my pain has been the worst out there, but I was left with some scars. Tyler was the blue in my sky, the jelly to my peanut butter, the burger to my fries, the syrup to my pancakes and the sugar to my tea. You catch the drift, and I'm not exaggerating, because he was all of this and much more to me. When he left, the hurt was so great that it stopped me from functioning properly. After attending church together for almost a year with no dialogue other than it being ministry related, we became friends following one of his little corny jokes at choir practice. For the next four years, we became exceptionally close and I thought nothing could break our bond.

We never put a title to the friendship, but every-one knew that one day we would eventually be together. Our parents, friends and even our pastor would talk about us ending up together. Tyler was my go-to guy for everything, and other than God, my world revolved around him. He never made a commitment to me per se, but we would talk about being in each other's future, and that was enough for me. I didn't want to pressure him about putting a label on what we had, because I was secure in our friendship/relationship knowing that at some point in the future we would get married.

I dived into a deeper intimacy with him without a promise. Allowing him to meet all my emotional needs and treating him like a boyfriend even though he wasn't. I was only setting myself up for a brutal fall. I shared my dreams, hopes, fears, past hurts and struggles. He knew everything about me and so did I about him – the good, the bad, and the ugly.

In late 2011, I realized that Tyler was beginning to pull away from me emotionally and physically, we went from spending nearly every day together and telling each other everything, to me having to schedule time to see him because he was that busy. I questioned him regularly about his behavior, but he said nothing was wrong; he was simply slacking in his schoolwork and needed to apply himself more. I readily accepted his response because I knew how much Bible school meant to him and how much he wanted to make his dad proud.

I remember going to church one Sunday excited to see him because I hadn't laid eyes on him in a week, but my excitement soon turned into months of weeping. While we were on stage preparing to minister in song, he bent down and whispered shyly, "Sam, we need to talk." Before I could interject to find out what was wrong, the choirmaster shooed us to get into position. Whatever it was, it would have to wait.

I was anxious for church to be over not knowing that what I was about to be told would damage my soul for a long time. When church was over, I searched around for Tyler and found him in the back with Pastor Hope and a young lady by his side. As I slowly approached the trio, my knees started to buckle, but I pushed my way forward. Tyler's eyes then made contact with mine and he bowed his head as if he was embarrassed. I could tell that he was uncomfortable because he started to fidget. Pastor Hope saw me on my way over to them and quickly ran off into the car park. I immediately knew something was not right.

When I finally reached Tyler, my universe came tumbling down with just five words "This is my girlfriend, Olivia." Without hesitation, I slapped Tyler in the face with all the strength I could muster and walked away from the duo. I knew the others who lingered in church after service saw me acting inappropriately, but I didn't care. I could hear Tyler shouting my name as he ran behind me, but took flight and headed into the car. I was broken because I believed in him, I believed in us and he stripped it away without having the courtesy to inform that he had a girlfriend. I was the closest person to him, but the last to know that he had replaced me. All the butterflies in my stomach died instantly; the one person who I thought would never hurt me was the one person who did.

Tyler called me every day trying to explain himself, but I never answered. He took the very best of me and left me with nothing; I felt empty and alone. It's one thing to have someone hurt you and not be around them, but we attended the same church, and so I had to see him even though I didn't want to. I had to adjust to life without him and it was hard. One of the most grueling things I had to go through was loving someone who had rejected me for someone else. Countless nights as I placed my head on my pillow, I had to speak life over myself; I had to command my soul to trust in the Lord because I felt like a balloon with no air – deflated.

Even though Tyler did me dirty, I deceived myself because my emotions were not submitted to God. I had created my own storm and got upset when it rained; well, scratch that, I got upset when it poured. When the revelation hit me I couldn't take it; I was the reason for the sadness I was going through. He didn't hurt me, my expectations did. If I had not allowed my expectations to run rampant I would have saved myself a bunch of heartbreak. Just like the Geico ad says, *"I just saved a bunch of money on my car insurance by by switching to Geico"* If I had switched to keeping my emotions on a leash from the beginning, I would have been saved from the pain.

One of the reasons we as get our hearts broken is because we defraud ourselves. In order for us to stop defrauding ourselves we need to quit being dumb and walk in discernment and discipline to avoid a disaster. Tyler never made a commitment to me, but I allowed it; giving him my all even though he never verbally promised me anything. I had spent so much time blaming him that I never thought to look at me. I had to stop wasting time and feeling sorry for myself and notice the blessings in my life and thank God for them. Yes, something was taken from me, but I had so many other things that I needed to be grateful for. I saw this encouragement piece on the internet and it changed my whole thinking.

"If you have $86,400 in your bank account and someone stole $10 from you, would you be upset and throw away the $86,390 in hopes of getting back at the person who took your $10? Or will you move on and live?" Well, a lot of us are throwing away the best parts of our lives because of the 10 percent of pain someone has caused. They are 86,400 seconds in every day, so why should I then allow what happened to ruin the rest of the 86,390. I decided to forgive Tyler so I could move on. It's one thing to say we want to be healed, but we have to fight for it. Jesus is always willing to heal, just like He was with the leper in Luke chapter 5, but we have a part to play. I had to bring more than an, "I forgive him" to the table, I had to really get up each day and choose to forgive him. I had to choose not to respond to the rejection in a sinful way. The Bible says to be angry and sin not.

Be angry, and do not sin. Meditate within your heart on your bed, and be still. Psalm 4:4

Yes, the sting of rejection often tried to run me over but I fought long and strong. I was determined not to be over-thrown. Jesus understood the pain of rejection, He came to His own and they did not receive him. He was nailed to the cross, bruised, exposed and betrayed. If He could forgive the very ones who rejected him, then so could I. The right thing to do is never easy. Yes, there were times I wanted to crawl back into my cocoon of unforgiveness, but God wouldn't let me. In 2012, I realized that I had truly forgiven Tyler. Whenever I saw him, instead of sucking my teeth and being nasty, I greeted him and even with a smile. I know you may say it's cliché and everyone says it. But I truthfully felt as though a load was lifted from my shoulders. God doesn't only heal physically but he heals us emotionally as well. If it had not been for Him I don't know where I would be.

"Healing doesn't mean that the damage never existed. It means the damage no longer controls our lives." - Unknown

When I stopped giving the damage power to control my life, I started to live again. Through deciding to live again is when God created a new chapter in my life. Or should I say a new chapter with an old twist. In 2013, when God told me who I would marry, I nearly choked on the sandwich I was eating. "Hell to the nah" my voice echoed in my living room that afternoon. In the beginning, I thought I wasn't hearing right, but when I heard His voice again, I knew it was my Shepherd speaking. As much as the enemy presents a counterfeit, God's voice is always known, whether we want to hear it or not. My voice dropped a decibel and I proceeded to talk to God.

"But why?" I asked.

"Because he's ready now; your timing isn't Mine." I heard His clear reply.

By now I'm guessing you've figured out where I'm going with this. Boy, was I seriously blown away. God told me that His plans were for me and Tyler to be together all along. Talk about revelation after revelation! The Lord started to download into my spirit. He showed me that Tyler had become an idol to me and He needed me to want Him more. I hadn't realized it, but at some point in our friendship, I placed Tyler in the position only God should fill, and God doesn't do too well with idolatry. The Bible speaks about how much He detests it. He also told me that he needed to work out some things in Tyler before he could become the husband He had ordained him to be.

About a month after God spoke to me, Tyler approached me after church and poured his heart out. Little did I know that after three months of being with Olivia he had broken it off. He told me he was confused and afraid and acted out of stupidity, which in turn caused me pain. I could see the sincerity in his eyes but I still wasn't letting him off the hook so easily. I knew what God had told me about us being together, but that didn't mean I should walk into anything with my eyes closed again. I did what I should have done from the very beginning and I asked him upfront about his intentions. He simply said, "To marry you, Samantha." The guy who broke me was the same one who I gave my heart back to again.

I had to leave fear by the side of the road on the trash heap and decide to love again. I grabbed Tyler with both hands, but I allowed God to lead and not my emotions. This year has been three years we have been married and I can say that I made the right choice when I said "I do". God truly blessed me when he placed him in my life. Tyler usually still apologizes for what he did, but as I usually tell him, "The breaking was a blessing". My past is a place of reference and not a place of residence; I would never hold him in bondage to his mistakes.

Tyler is still the blue in my sky, the jelly to my peanut butter, the burger to my fries, the syrup to my pancakes and the sugar to my tea, but God is my all in all and Tyler is okay with that, because that's how it's supposed to be. We are now expecting our first child and I wouldn't trade my family for anything. If I had refused to forgive Tyler, I would have missed out on what I have today; my stubbornness would have halted all that God wanted to work out in both our lives. We never have to manipulate or force an outcome; we just have to trust God to open the right doors at the right time.

My heart should have been guarded until God told me it was time to let someone in. Unlike me, you can avoid heartbreak more effectively by keeping a rein on your emotions. Set boundaries so your heart can be guarded from unnecessary pain. You only have one heart, so take care of it.

Confession #9

A Second Chance

"A broken heart is like getting shampoo in your eyes. It feels for a while like you'll never see again, but after a few tears you get over it."
- Mark Amend

Even though I believe this now, at the time when I was going through an unfavorable circumstance, it would have been difficult to agree with this quote. I cried way more than a few tears. Mark Amend should have probably said 'after a few years' because that was me. I thought I would never see again.

It was a match made in heaven when I met Elizabeth, or Lizzy as I often called her. From the moment we met, I knew she would become my wife. She was quiet, gentle in spirit, kind, conscientious and would always put the needs of others above her own. Notwithstanding her quiet personality, she was a lioness when it came to the things of the Lord and she loved and served Him wholeheartedly.

Her passion for God was highly infectious and attractive. God had blessed me with a rare gem and I always found the time to thank Him for her.

We got married after courting for a year and it was the happiest day of my life. We were doing well in our careers, functioning in our church, moved into our first home debt-free by the favor of God and just basking in the newlywed glory. We both wanted to have a large family so when we found out she was pregnant after six months into our marriage, we were overjoyed. But that joy was short lived for me, because only a week after she had barged into our bedroom to surprise me with the pregnancy test, she was gone.

While waiting for Elizabeth to come home from her women's ministry meeting, I heard a pounding on the door. It was odd for anyone to be banging at such an odd hour in our neighborhood, so I speedily went to see who was there. Two police officers were standing on our doorstep and I knew straightaway that something was wrong. They refused to look me in the eyes; the look on their faces had already told a tragic story I wasn't ready to hear.

"There was a head on collision on the highway, and I'm sorry to notify you, but your wife was killed on impact."

All I heard was 'killed on impact' anything before or after that was all a blur. I shook my head in disbelief as I grabbed on to the doorframe for support. There are no human words possible to explain how I felt; it was as if they had physically ripped my heart from my chest. Sudden destruction came upon me as labor pains upon a pregnant person. My Lizzy and our baby were gone, and I was beyond devastated.

You're more than likely asking yourself who broke his heart that he couldn't forgive and move on? One word – God. I blamed God for what happened to Lizzy that night. How could a Father who said He loved me, take the very thing I loved more than myself? How could that same loving Father allow the sweetest person to be killed in such a horrific way, especially after coming from doing His work? What made me more livid was the fact that Elizabeth was hit by a drunken driver who survived with minor injuries. Ludicrous!

As the hatred, unforgiveness and resentment grew in my heart, I stopped going to church. It felt as if I was walking around with tiny shards of glass in my chest; the pain was that unbearable. I wanted to turn to God, but I felt betrayed; the very God who said He would never forsake His children, had forsaken me. As my faith decreased, the depression increased.

The nightmares were haunting and I had to fight away the suicidal thoughts. Before I knew it, a month had turned into six, and six months had turned into a year, and I was still being swallowed by the depression. My friends and family eventually stopped coming by, but I knew it was because of my bitterness and the fact that they didn't know what to say to me. Heartbreak is a feeling you truly can't understand until it happens to you. They wanted to help, but didn't know where to start, and neither did I.

Mental illness is prevalent, and we as Christians need to be educated on such things lest people succumbed to it right under our noses. Simply telling a person 'just pray' when they are mentally incapable won't do much. Somewhere in the world right now, a Christian is contemplating suicide for whatever reason and we need to be properly educated and taught how to deal with such matters. Yes, prayer works from the spiritual aspect, but practicality is always very useful.

I was at the end of the rope, holding on for dear life but still wanting to let go, and that's when Rachel entered the picture. God literally sent me an angel in human form to help me; she was the vessel God used to bring some of my greatest healing. Rachel moved in next door about five months after my wife died, but I never took notice because I was wallowing in grief. She would try to greet me in passing, but I often acted like the Grinch. I didn't steal Christmas but something had been stolen from me. I remember the first conversation we had that literally left me voiceless.

"Hey, good morning Jason," she said cheerfully on her way to her car.

"What's so good about the morning?" I grumbled, wondering how she knew my name.

She turned around and looked me dead in the eyes. "You know, some people die at twenty-five and aren't buried until seventy-five, don't let that be you. God comforts those who are willing to be comforted."

Many people had been trying to get through to me since Lizzy's death. But what came out of Rachel's mouth that afternoon changed my life completely; something so simple yet so profound. It made me think back to the kind of person Elizabeth was, and I knew she wouldn't have wanted me to live in self-pity and turn away from God as I had done. She would have wanted me to live in reckless abandonment for God regardless of the storms of life, and her death wasn't an exception. In John chapter 11:38-44 speaks about the story of Lazarus. After Jesus had spoken the word and told him to come forth, Lazarus opened his eyes and came out of the tomb. But even though he was now alive he was still bound; he was alive, but he was restricted.

Verse 44 says; *And he who had died came out bound hand and foot with grave clothes, and his face was wrapped with a cloth. Jesus said to them, "Loose him, and let him go"*

Even though I was alive I was bound and it was impossible for me to live unless I made the decision to throw off the grave clothes. I had to cut away the restrictions; I had to cut away the bitterness, the sorrow, the self-pity, the hatred, the unforgiveness and the blame game. Jesus wanted to loose me and let me go into joy, peace, love, forgiveness and freedom. Unlike Lazarus who had people to take his clothes off, I had to do it on my own.

I had gone from the presence of God for so long, but when I came back it was as if I never left; the love of the Father makes you feel that way. I took my cares and threw them on the Lord instead of carrying them all, and I found the comfort in Him I was looking for. He is the God who comforted me in my tribulation and paved a way for me to comfort those who are also troubled.

Blessed be the God and Father of our Lord Jesus Christ, the Father of mercies and God of all comfort, who comforts us in all our tribulation, that we may be able to comfort those who are in any trouble, with the comfort with which we ourselves are comforted by God. 2 Corinthians 1:3-4

You will know when you've been healed from a wound, because when you touch it, it doesn't hurt. It means you can see or think about that person and you can still breathe. Whenever I would think about Lizzy I started to laugh and remember our good times instead of crying about the fact that she was no longer with me. I had to trust that if God took her away then He did it with all reason.

I eventually became friends with Rachel and she played an active part in my journey of healing; she brought calm in the times of stress. At the end of the second year of Elizabeth's death, our friendship deepened and my feelings for her grew, but I was afraid. After shutting myself from the world for so long, it was a bit challenging to open my heart again. "What if I get too close and she gets taken away as well?" were my thoughts. But God didn't give us the spirit of fear, so that meant that it was from the devil himself.

The future is unknown and no one can tell it but God, so why should we be afraid of what we do not know instead of living in the now and what we do know? If I wanted a second chance at love I had to choose faith instead of fear, and I chose faith. The thing is, experiencing love exposes us to hurt, and I had to take the risk of being hurt so that I could love again.

Today marks 15 years that we have been together and 12 years of marriage. We have three wonderful children and I adore my wife and love her unconditionally. Instead of being deterred by my brokenness and fear, she showed me that it was okay to love again. I am honored that God gave me this special gift.

My time spent with Elizabeth was great and I will always have the memories of our short life together. I count myself blessed to have had something that was so hard to say goodbye to. Even in her death she brought people to Christ. The young lady who crashed into Lizzy that night gave her life to the Lord and to this day is still a Christian. I honestly believe that if Elizabeth knew beforehand that her death would turn someone to God, she would have have willingly said "Yes."

Just as Job said, the Lord gives and the Lord takes away, but blessed be the name of the Lord. God was with me, both in the storm and in the peace. At my saddest, He was my comforter and He can do the same for you. War changes people, but you decide how it changes you. Living by your hurt instead of your heart is a recipe for bitterness and destruction. Don't put your heart in cardiac arrest while you're still alive, allow it to keep beeping.

Hurt With Hope

The world's definition of hope and the biblical definition of the hope we have are not the same. Someone once said, "Where the world understands hope as wishful thinking, Christians see hope as a **'know so'** and not a **'hope so'**." A believer knows that his hope is solid and firm because it is based on God's word. The Bible encourages us countless times to wait on God expectantly in the harsh times, knowing that He will turn things around. Even in the most severe of times we need to learn how to hurt with hope instead of hurting hopelessly.

When you pass through the waters, I will be with you; and when you pass through the rivers, they will not sweep over you. When you walk through the fire, you will not be burned; the flames will not set you ablaze. Isaiah 43:2 You have to see it before you see it. Did you get that? Give your physical eyes a break and move with eyes of faith. You have to see your breakthrough even before you see it. God said the river will not sweep you over and the fire will not burn you. It's quite difficult at times to stop looking with your physical eyes, but what choice do you really have? If the flames are that high and that intense, it means that the only person who can pull you out is God, so why not trust Him? Why not place your hope in Him? So you're asking the question, "How can I count it all joy in various trials?"

Instead of seeing your suffering as something to escape, rest in His strength, power and comfort, knowing that He will be true to His word.

Sometimes in order for us to reach our destiny, we need the hurt and the giants of life. David needed Goliath in order to reach the throne. This young boy had his hope rooted so deep in God that despite his weakness, he fought with a giant who was guaranteed by man to take him out. The fight was set and all the money was on Goliath to be victorious, but that did not put a damper on David's mood. He saw his victory through faith even before it was manifested physically.

"Then David said to Saul, Let no man's heart fail because of him; this servant will go and fight with this Philistine." 1 Samuel 17:32

David knew that the same God, who saved him from the paw of the lion and the paw of the bear, would save him from the hand of the Philistine. His faith and hope were so strong, that he went out to battle without any armor. The odds weren't in his favor but the little boy with his sling and five smooth stones defeated and utterly destroyed the giant. Do not let your heart fail today because of your situation; yes, the odds may be against you, but victory is with the one who hopes in the Lord. The uncircumcised Philistine in your life WILL NOT slaughter you. Fear not; it's going to work out in your favor.

There is a difference between **'mind full'** and being **'mindful'**. Right now your mind is filled with worry, frustration, defeat, stress and pain. It's full of everything that is negative which can cause feelings of hopelessness; your giant is beginning to look bigger than usual. But I want you to be mindful of this thing, God said: "I will be with you in the storm, I will deliver you from your enemies, I will not leave you, Do not be dismayed, for those who are with you are more than those against you, I will restore you, I will lift you up." The Lord has never lied before and He will not start today.

You need to also hurt with the hope that one day you will love again. Don't become so damaged that when someone wants to finally give you what you deserve you don't know how to respond. If you want to have a deep connection, then you have to be vulnerable, so don't allow yourself to be turned into a robot. You are tempered with the spine of steel. Yes, you've been hurt but you're still standing here today. As was said in the previous confession, "Don't die while you're still alive."

Stop wallowing in the thick pile of self-pity, shake off your sullen mood and get to healing. Sail with the Master; I'm pretty sure you've weathered storms with Him before. If you only knew how resilient you are and how faithful your God is you wouldn't bother about your present predicament.

Ask God to cease the discomfort, and if He doesn't, then ask Him to bring peace in the discomfort.

The Bible says all we need is faith as small as a mustard seed. But listen to this; even though a mustard seed is exceptionally small, when matured, it reaches an average height of between 6 and 20 feet with a 20-foot spread. If God says that a mustard seed faith can move mountains then what would the mustard tree faith do? If we are to fight and win the battles that life throws our way, our faith and hope need to be bigger than the mustard seed.

God has spoken to Satan on your behalf and has said "Thus far and no further." Psalm119:71 states *"It is good for me that I have been afflicted, that I may learn Your statutes."* He is building you even when it feels like you're being broken. Fight the fire you're up against with the Holy Ghost fire and you are guaranteed to win. Be undisturbed, unbothered and unmoved; lift your eyes to hills from whence cometh your help and know what it means to hurt with hope.

Though the fig tree may not blossom, Nor fruit be on the vines; Though the labor of the olive may fail, and the fields yield no food; Though the flock may be cut off from the fold, And there be no herd in the stalls Yet I will rejoice in the Lord, I will joy in the God of my salvation. Habakkuk 3:17-18

A Pearl Emerges

It is said that the pearl is a product of suffering and pain; depicting a phenomenal story about turning the trash of life into something incredible. A foreign substance slips into the soft flesh of the oyster's shell; it irritates the oyster and its natural reaction is to cover up the irritant to protect itself. When the irritant is covered and the wound heals, and the pearl forms.

This is the same with us; had there been no wounding there would be no pearl. Life has thrown some sand your way to cause pain and sorrow, but if allowed, God can make the rarest of a pearl out of the affliction. You are strong because you've been weak and you are wise because you've been foolish. It's not about what you lost, but about what you have left over. So shout Hallelujah and thank God for the leftovers. Thank God for the irritants of life that made you into the pearl you are today. *"Those who dive into the sea of affliction bring up rare pearls."* -Charles Spurgeon

For the ones who are going through a rough time right now, I want to leave you with a little encouragement. God is breathing on your situation right now; rest in that fact. Someone told me, "Do not misunderstand the existence of darkness for the absence of God." Just because you don't feel Him in the midst of your storm doesn't mean God isn't there. He is there even in your darkness. Genesis Chapter 1:2 says, *The earth was without form, and void; and darkness was on the face of the deep. And the Spirit of God was hovering over the face of the waters.* Catch that revelation and run with it; God is active even in the dark. I want you to run the race with endurance; have the ability to hang on even when it's easier to give up. Say it with me – **"No grit, No pearl."**

To the ones who have been injured along the way of life and find it hard to let go, understand that in this broken world, relationships can get messy for different reasons and end in tragedy, but in the presence of Jesus there will always be healing. The past is the past; there is no reason to keep reliving it. Stop making it your favorite movie that you keep on replay. Trees are experts at letting things go; when another season comes you never see them trying to hold on to what was, instead, they accept what is and go with the flow. And can I say that each season is remarkable in its own way? It makes more sense to live in the present tense. "Stop being a prisoner of your past and become the architect of your future." –Robin Sharma. Suffering only adds character to one's appearance, while making us more beautiful than before.

There is a difference when a person does a thorough clean from when they do a light cleaning. Every day in our homes we do a light clean. This is where we sweep, wipe, mop and clean the places that are visible. However, when we do a thorough cleaning, we usually pull away the sofa, the refrigerator, the bed etc., so we can get to every ounce of dust and filth behind the scene that have accumulated over time.

Healing properly reminds me of this. In your healing process you need to be true to yourself. It is not a time for a light cleaning, but the master cleaning of all cleanings needs to be done to get rid of every and anything that can be a stumbling block. Ask God to reveal the places where the hurt, pain, betrayal and the unforgiveness reside that you cannot see. Ask Him to peel back your world and disclose the things you don't want to see. A pearl may just be hiding behind the bed you are unwilling to get behind and clean thoroughly.

"Dear scarred and beautiful soul, even with your wounds you are flawless. I speak to every physical, mental, and emotional pain. I speak life to your inner man and I declare that the battle will not destroy you. May the Almighty God overshadow you on your journey. I pray that God floods your soul with such joy that you will look past the negative and see the positive in your situation. Tragedy is part of the human experience but being defeated is optional, so what will you choose? Allow a pearl to emerge from the oyster and let God turn your trauma into triumph."

Confession Time!

God has always used broken people and He can do the same with you. Elijah was suicidal, Rahab was a prostitute and Mary Magdalene was demon-possessed. You have read the different stories in this book and have seen the transformation that has taken place in the lives of these once scarred souls; their testing is now their testimony. Revelation Chapter 12 says we have overcome by the blood of the Lamb and the word of our testimony.

I want to challenge you to take the time to sit quietly and write out your confession about how you moved from trauma to triumph. When you are finished, ask God to use your story for His glory to bring healing to someone and that He would reveal such persons. Your story may not be written in a book, but it will surely play its part in touching lives. By faith you overcame and you can now help someone else do the same. It's time to confess!